my first visit to
a farm

English translation © Copyright 1990 by Barron's Educational Series, Inc.

© Parramón Ediciones, S.A.
First Edition, 1990
The title of the Spanish edition is *mi primera visita a la granja*

All rights reserved.
No part of this book may be reproduced in any form, by photostat, microfilm, xerography, or any other means, or incorporated into any information retrieval system, electronic or mechanical, without the written permission of the copyright owner.

All inquiries should be addressed to:
Barron's Educational Series, Inc.
250 Wireless Boulevard
Hauppauge, New York 11788

Library of Congress Catalog Card No. 89-17985.

International Standard Book No. 0-8120-4305-7

Library of Congress Cataloging-in-Publication Data

Parramón, José María.
 [Mi primera visita a la granja. English]
 My first visit to a farm /J.M. Parramón, G. Sales.—1st ed.
   p. cm.
 Translation of: Mi primera visita a la granja.
 Summary: A class and its teacher visit a farm where they learn about such animals as cows, chickens, pigs, sheep, and rabbits.
 ISBN 0-8120-4305-7
 1. Domestic animals—Juvenile literarue. 2. Farms—Juvenile literature.
[1. Domestic animals. 2. Farms] I. Sales G. II. Title.
SF75.P3613 1990   89-17985
636—dc20   CIP
                                  AC

Printed in Spain by EMSA, Barcelona.
L.D.: B-38.488-89

9012 9960 987654321

my first visit to
a farm

G. Sales

J.M. Parramón

New York • Toronto • Sydney

One day in class John, Mary, Peter, and Susan noticed a new poster on the wall. On it were some rabbits, a cow, a sheep, and several other animals.

"These are all tame or domestic animals," the teacher said. "Tomorrow we're going to go to a farm to see them."

The farm was a long way from the city. It was surrounded by woods and fields.

The teacher told them a lot of things about the farm. "These dogs guard the entrance and protect the other animals."

"The farm cats also have an important job. They chase the mice that steal the grain."

"The horses help by pulling the carts and heavy wagons."

"This is the barn for the cows. The farmer is milking one of them."

"In the pigpen the pigs never stop eating and grunting."

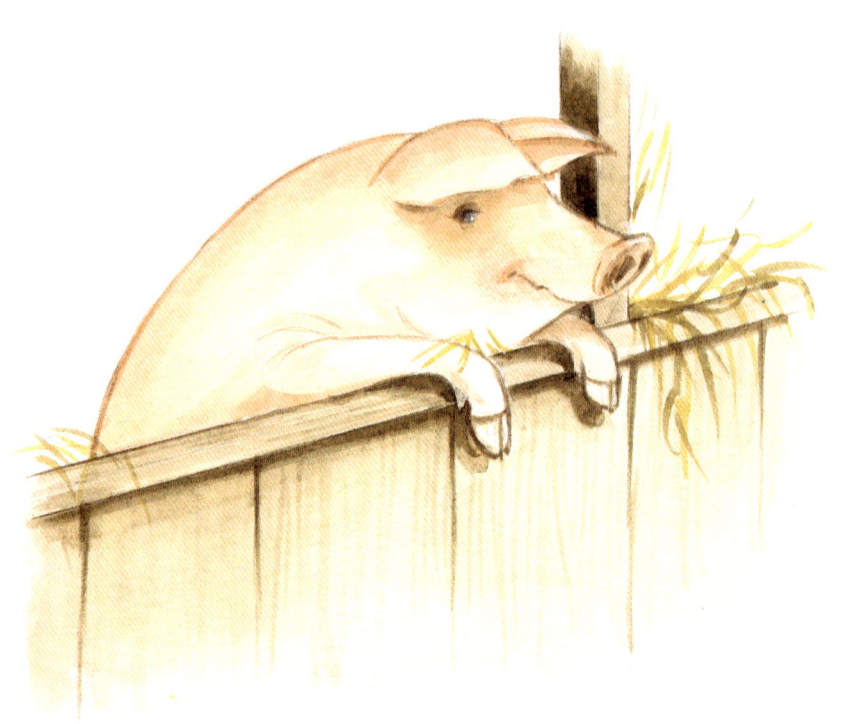

"A herd of cattle and a flock of sheep are playing in the meadow. Can you see the sheepdog that is keeping them together?" asked the teacher.

"The rabbit nibbles on the carrot, the ducks swim around the pond, and the pigeons fly in and out of their little house."

"The rooster and some of the hens run around the barnyard pecking for food."

"But some of the hens sit on their nests and lay eggs. The farmer's wife is collecting them."

"What a beautiful, fresh egg!" exclaimed John.

"Just look at all the newly-hatched chicks," said Peter.

"Aren't they soft and fluffy," exclaimed Susan.

Mary agreed and she added, "I'll never forget *my first visit to a farm!*"

FOR PARENTS AND TEACHERS

MY FIRST VISIT TO A FARM

Domestic Animals

Humans have had many different reasons for keeping domestic animals. In ancient times wild animals were captured and put in pens to provide food, leather, and wool. Later, people discovered that the manure of animals could be used to return fertility to the soil. Still later, oxen and horses were used as beasts of burden and as means of transport. Horses were also used for military purposes, first to pull warriors in chariots and later to carry knights into battle.

For thousands of years animals have also been trained to assist hunters, to protect life and property, and to be pleasant companions for children and adults.

But the use of domestic animals is not the same in all parts of the world and depends a great deal on cultural habits and the availability of particular species. For example, the elephant is considered a domestic animal in India, and the same is true of the yak in Tibet. Other native species that have been domesticated in the parts of the world where they are found are the llama in Peru and Bolivia, the camel in the deserts of Africa and Asia, and the reindeer in the Arctic region.

Farm Animals

Domestic animals that are raised to provide food, leather, fur, or wool, or are used for agricultural tasks are sometimes called farm animals.

Domestic fowl, or poultry, include chickens, kept for their meat and eggs; turkeys, for their abundant meat; ducks and geese, for their meat and also for their fine underfeathers, called *down*.

The ruminants, or animals that chew their cud, include cows—which are raised for their meat, milk (used to make butter, cheese, and yogurt), and skins (used to make leather) and sheep and goats—which are raised for their meat, skins, hair, and milk. Horses, donkeys, and mules help with work on the farm.

It could be said that we use every part of pigs except their grunting. Their meat is made into products like ham, bacon, and sausages; their fat is used to make lard and soap; their hair is made into brushes; their skin into leather; and their bones are used in the manufacture of industrial glues.

Rabbits, which are raised for their meat, reproduce very rapidly and are able to adapt to very different climates.

The Reproduction of Farm Animals

Poultry incubate eggs in which the embryos develop, but the rest of the farm animals are mammals—that is, animals that give birth directly to offspring that have previously developed inside the mother's body and have received nutritional substances through the mother's blood.

The gestation periods of farm animals vary considerably from one species to another. Mares give birth to their foals after eleven months of gestation; cows give birth to their calves after nine months; sheep and goats give birth to lambs and kids after five months. But all the young are able to stand up a few hours after birth and can run after their mothers to feed on the milk from their mothers' mammary glands.

The Traditional Farm

The traditional idea of a farm is of a family unit dedicated to the raising of livestock and the cultivation of crops. The family can then live on the products of their crops and the meat, eggs, and milk produced by their livestock. Some of the livestock also help with the cultivation of crops.

Family farms still exist even in the developed countries, but today they concentrate on raising fruit and/or vegetables, grain, and dairying. Barnyard animals may still be raised to provide meat and eggs for the family or for sale in local markets.

Industrial Farms

Unlike family farms, industrial farms specialize in the intensive raising of one particular plant or animal species in order to obtain high levels of productivity.

One of the most developed kinds of industrial farm is the egg farm. The use of cross-breeding has produced extremely disease-resistant and productive breeds. Productivity is then further enhanced by the use of scientifically formulated feeds and regulated lighting that prolong the hours during which the hens lay eggs.

Another kind of highly developed industrial farm is the dairy, which has become a virtual "milk factory." Automatic systems fill the feed troughs, milk the cows, and collect the milk. Cattle raising—which includes both milk-cows and cattle kept solely for their meat—is one of humanity's major sources of food.